Life Story

ISBN-13: 978-0-9970298-8-8

First edition: December 2016
Updated edition: October 2018

Published in the United States of America
1 2 3 4 5 6 7 8 9 10

A Quick Introduction

"We'll never get to our ideal life destination, if we don't define the road to get there."

Every day our actions are writing a page in our story. By writing the ending of our story ahead of time, we can build a daily plan that makes that end a reality.

I created *Life Story* out of necessity. I needed a plan for my life, and the best way to have one, I thought, was by intentionally writing the story I wanted to live. You may have heard the adage "Your life is one big story filled with many chapters." However, did you know that we have the ability to write that story, chapter by chapter? In fact, if we don't write it with intentionality, we're setting ourselves up for an uncertain ending, at best.

Sure, there will be edits and rewrites along the way, and you certainly can't predict the future. But, if you don't write the story you want for your life, you're guaranteed to get an unpredictable result.

What are your values?
What is your purpose?
What should your goals be?
Do you have a life question?
Do you want your life to matter, but not know where to start?
Are you concerned you might not leave the legacy you want?
Do you feel overwhelmed by all of these questions?

Don't be. These are questions that can be answered by writing your life story and I've put together this step-by-step guide to make it as simple as possible.

You'll find your purpose, priorities, values, goals, and guardrails. All the tools you need to write the story you want are in this guide. All you have to do is fill in the blanks.

Your life story is being written as we speak. Now you can take control of what's being written.

How It Works

There are 10 lessons at the beginning of this guide. Read each lesson, then complete the corresponding section in your life story.

As you go through this process, think of me as the ghostwriter on your journey. However, you are the author. I've taken the liberty of writing an outline for your life story, but it's in your hands to fill in the blanks. <u>As you write the story, imagine yourself at the end of your life reflecting on how you lived.</u>

Lesson 1: The Preface

Instructions: *Read the lesson and complete the section titled "The Preface" on page 26.*

One of the most important questions we can ask before starting anything is *why?* Far too often we skip over the exercise of asking why and jump right into doing or not doing. However, without a well-understood why, our effort often gets lost in the minutiae of everyday life. So, why *Life Story*? When we have a million and one other things to do, why is this exercise worth our time? The answer lies in the power of *definition*. Albert Einstein once said, "If I were given one hour to save the world, I would spend 59 minutes defining the problem and one minute solving it."

We'll never have the life we want if we don't first define exactly what that life is and then create a clear roadmap that gets us there. And that is what *Life Story* does for us. **Every day our actions are writing a page in our story.** By writing the ending of our story first, we can then build a daily plan that will make that finish line a reality. I created *Life Story* out of necessity. I needed a plan for my life, and the best way to have one, I thought, was by intentionally writing the story I wanted to live. You may have heard the adage "Your life is one big story filled with many chapters." However, did you know that we have the ability to write that story, chapter by chapter? Sure, there will be edits and rewrites along the way, and you certainly can't predict the future. But, if you don't write the story you want for your life, you're guaranteed to get an unpredictable result.

What are your values? What is your purpose? What goals should you have? Do you have a life question? Do you want your life to matter, but don't know where to start? Are you concerned you might not leave the legacy you want? Do you feel overwhelmed by all of these questions? Don't be. These are questions that can be answered by writing your life story. And since the idea of writing a life story may seem overwhelming, the *Life Story* study guide is designed to make it as simple as possible. In this guide and corresponding lessons, you will find every tool you need to write the story you want. This is a step-by-step program that will walk you through defining your purpose, priorities, goals, and guardrails. You just have to fill in the blanks! Your life story is being written as we speak. Now you can take control it.

Here's how it works: As you go through this process, think of yourself as the author and me as the ghostwriter. I've taken the liberty of writing an outline for your life story, but it's in your hands to fill in the blanks. As you write the story, imagine yourself at the end of your life reflecting on how you lived. This will allow you to look beyond your present circumstances and focus on your desired future. By doing that, you'll soon see what you need to do *today* to make it happen. *I encourage you to immerse yourself in the process.* **You're a writer whether you like it or not, and this will be the most important story you ever write**. But don't get overwhelmed. Remember, it doesn't have to be perfect. You can edit and rewrite as much as you need.

If you are married or want to do this exercise with a significant other, feel free; however, if you have the time, start by doing it on your own. Then, bring your stories together and write a combined one. Though your life story is intertwined with your spouse or significant other, you will still have things that are unique to you.

The writer Mark Batterson once said, "A change of pace and a change of place equals a change of perspective." If you're able, do this exercise away from your normal daily routine. Although it isn't impossible, it can be challenging to dream outside of the box when surrounded by our typical environment and distractions. Go to a park, a new coffee shop, or take a day away if you can, and work on your life story. An act as simple as a new location can be invaluable to your dreaming process. If that isn't feasible for you, that's okay. The most important thing is that you write your life story, which brings me to the most important thing you could do today.

Schedule

Mark the calendar for time to go through the *Life Story* process. Just hoping you'll find the time to write your life story will leave you discouraged because it won't happen. You won't write it. My most significant step in the process of writing my first book was scheduling time to write that book on my calendar. How long should it take? It depends. It could take a few hours, a day, or more. It just depends on you. I recommend setting aside a few hours at a time to work on this. Then, take a break and come back. However, before you finish working on *Life Story* each time, schedule your next time to work on it. Never stop the *Life Story* process without first scheduling the next time to work on it. So, figure out when you're going to work on *Life Story* right now. Mark it on your calendar, get a babysitter, or postpone watching your "show." Make it a priority and get time on the calendar today. Or if you're free now… start writing!

Application: *Complete the section titled "The Preface" on page 26.*

Lesson 2: Life Question

Instructions: *Read the lesson and complete the section titled "Life Question" on page 27.*

A question. What's so intriguing and powerful about a question? After all, it's just a series of words put together with a funny-looking symbol tacked on the end. Right? I've found that a question can be one of the most powerful tools we have in our arsenal. Questions change the course of our lives. Here are a couple of examples:

Will you marry me?
Should we go to war?
Do you want to have kids?
Should we buy that house?
What's the diagnosis?

I could go on and on with the questions, but it's easy to see how the answer to any of these questions would shape and change someone, and probably many someones with the ever so simplest of answers. **It's a question that has the ability to dig under our skin and go to the deepest parts of our heart to find an answer.** A question is something like a detective that, when allowed to penetrate our wall of insecurities, can bring forth life and clarity in a way that only moments before seemed to be miles away. Questions are powerful and the right question is life changing. This is why I believe every person should have a "life question."

A "life question" is a question that immediately gets to the center of who you are and who you want to be. When this question is created appropriately, it will bring immediate Focus, Inspiration, and Satisfaction. The beautiful thing about a life question is that it doesn't matter how many times it's asked, if you answer with honesty, it will clearly point you in the direction your heart desires to go. I think it's only fitting that the best way to create a life question is by asking yourself a series of questions. However, before we jump into those questions let me give a bit more context.

A life question is meant to be asked on a daily basis in order to guide you toward your purpose. It's a question that can be used to center and focus all of your efforts. Or it can be used to bring you peace and calm when you find yourself overwhelmed by everything that life entails and you don't know where to start. Remember, **your life question is a part of your life story and every story has edits and rewrites**.

One of the biggest mistakes you could make is putting too much pressure on creating a life question because you want it to be perfect. There's a pretty good chance that everyone's life question will change or be edited with time and that's perfectly okay.

To start your life question, I will give you two starting statements that may help you in creating your question. You don't have to start your question with these statements, but they can be helpful when creating your question. The first is:

What if I lived each day…
What if I lived each day as if my family was the only thing that mattered?
What if I lived each day as if nothing could stop me?
What If I lived each day putting others above myself?

And another example of a beginning statement you could find helpful:

What if the only thing that mattered today was…
What if the only thing that mattered today was taking one step toward being a better husband, wife, mom, dad, friend, colleague, etc.?
What if the only thing that mattered today was sharing love?

Hopefully by now you're starting to get some ideas around what your life question could be, but if you're still not sure, ask yourself these three questions.

1. What focuses me?
2. What inspires me?
3. What satisfies me?

Your life question should bring focus to your daily actions. It should inspire you to move forward. And answering it with confidence will bring a level of satisfaction that allows you to pat yourself on the back and say "good job today." You can also use these three questions to check your life question by asking yourself: Does this focus me? Does this inspire me? Does this satisfy me?

Once you've nailed down your life question, it's time to start implementing it into your life. Simply having a question doesn't change anything. So you need to do the following things on a daily basis:

1. **Ask it.** Send yourself an automated email, write it on your mirror, put it on your dash, tape it to your computer screen, make it your screensaver, set a calendar reminder. The point is to ask yourself this question every day and sometimes multiple times a day. If you never ask it, it's pointless to have it.

2. **Ponder it.** The process of thinking about the question and how it relates to what you have to do today is where creative magic happens. It's where you make life-altering decisions or simple adjustments to your routine that align with the life you want to live. Sometimes you may ponder all day and others it may be just a few seconds; either way give yourself time to think.

3. **Do it.** I think it goes without saying that we can ask and even ponder, but if we don't do anything about it, we're wasting our time. Doing can be big and it can be small. We don't have to "quit" our jobs every day, we just have to learn how to take the steps necessary that day in order to be moving in the direction our question points us.

So, what's your question? If you don't know it already, take some time today to come up with several options and start testing them using what I've taught you in this video. **Great questions demand great responses.** The answer to your question will be the story you write.

Application: *Complete the section titled "Life Question" on page 27.*

Lesson 3: Defining What's Important

Instructions: *Read the lesson and complete the section titled "Introduction: What's Important?" on page 28.*

Every day is an exercise in prioritizing what matters. This is true at every stage of our life, but becomes an even greater reality as we gain more independence. When we were young our parents prioritized our life and we needed that help. If my daughter were to prioritize her own life, the top of that list would probably be: get a snack, watch a show, more snack, another show, snack again, and so on. She's not yet capable of determining what matters, so we do it for her in the hopes that as she grows and gains more freedom, she will be able to prioritize the "important" things in life.

Everyone reading this has the freedom to choose their priorities. We each have the freedom to choose what's important in our lives. And even if you've never sat down and defined your priorities, you have determined them without even knowing it. Growing up in church, I would hear the phrase "You'll know where your heart is by looking at your checkbook and your calendar." As much as this phrase may have gotten old throughout the years, the principle behind it remains true. **Your actions are clear indicators of your priorities.**

Here's a quick mental exercise. Think about the actions you took every day for the last week, the money you spent, and the mental effort you exerted. Then bucket them into 10 categories labeled 1 through 10 in order of most time, money, and effort spent to least. Now that you have that list in your mind, mentally add a title to the top of that list. My list would say "Chris's Priorities." Now, imagine that list is the obituary that will be read aloud at your funeral. Are you happy with it?

Don't get discouraged if the answer is no. It most likely is no. Heck, it would be no for me most of the time too, and that's the point. We often have an image of the priorities we'd like to have in our mind but have never truly measured them against our time, money, and effort. And even if we have, it's easy to get off track. I've done an exercise like this with my wife several times a year for quite a few years and each time we find things in our life that need to be adjusted and that's perfectly normal. With the list we just created in mind, let's create the list we actually want for our life. In this section of *Life Story*, your goal is to write out a list of priorities. These are the important things that you want in your life; the cornerstones you would want to be read aloud at your funeral.

There is not a right or wrong number of priorities to list, but I've found 10 to be an average for most people. Honestly, the fewer you have the better, but with life comes many priorities.

My top 7 priorities look like this: Faith, Self, Wife, Kids, Friends, Career, Finances. I want to point out one thing that may strike you as interesting and it's my second priority, self. Self represents my health, growth, rest, etc. I take the same approach as the airlines do. If you don't take care of yourself, you won't be able to take care of anyone else.

Now, this doesn't mean that I finish eating before my family gets food, but it means that as a whole I need to make sure I'm personally healthy in order to bring balance to my other priorities.

You might ask: Why are we defining our priorities? The answer is two-fold. **Defining our priorities is the foundation to building the story we want for our life.** And if we don't first define what we value most in life, we won't know where to focus our time and energy; you wouldn't know the chapters in your book. The act of force ranking what is important in our lives really does three key things in the long term:

1. It helps us make better decisions by defining in what priority we should be making them. Decisions that adversely affect my top priorities now get correctly scrutinized.

2. It clarifies what to cut and what to keep. When we're deciding between giving more time to priority 1 or 7, we have a pretty clear answer.

3. It acts as a warning alarm for when we're getting off track. As we evaluate our time, money, and effort toward each of our priorities we can quickly see if an adjustment is needed.

Beyond needing a list of priorities to continue on the *Life Story* journey, you need a list to keep you focused on the life you want to live in general. Take some time today to rank your priorities. If you're having a hard time deciding between two priorities in your life, just go with your gut. Remember, we're writing a story and you can always edit if needed. However the biggest mistake is not writing it at all.

Application: *Complete the section titled "Introduction: What's Important?" on page 28.*

10

Lesson 4: Writing Chapters

Instructions: *Read the lesson and complete a "Chapter" for each of the priorities you created in the previous section. Use your list of priorities to create the title for each chapter. The "Chapters" section starts on page 30.*

Many authors first create an outline that serves as a guide on the journey of writing their book. Now that you have listed your priorities, you've done just that. You have created an outline for your life story and today we start writing the first chapters. There are multiple philosophies on what necessary components make up a chapter.

When I was writing *Step*, I talked to many professional writers as I was seeking the best writing method. One of those writers I talked to was a scriptwriter in Hollywood. I wanted my book to be a story, and I thought that talking to someone who wrote the entertaining stories we watch on TV for a living might have some great insight into how I should structure my chapters… and he did. At the time, he was writing TV shows for one of the big networks, and he explained how every show, just like every good book, had a theme that was repeated. In a TV show that theme is repeated in every episode, and in a book it's every chapter. **When you crack the code to the theme of your life story, writing the chapters becomes easy.** You're writing to a sequence and that rhythm keeps your reader engaged.

As you move through the "Chapter Templates" section of *Life Story*, you'll notice that each chapter has the exact same sequence. When you start writing your first chapter just follow the sequence laid out for you in the guide. We start writing each chapter of our life by telling our reader why this part of our life is important. For example if I were writing a chapter titled "Kids," it would read something like this: *Avery was important to me because she was my legacy. She was my biggest contribution to the world, and I loved her with everything inside of me.* The great thing about writing your life story is that it doesn't have to be grammatically perfect. It just needs to communicate a message that aligns with your heart.

Let's move on to the next part of the chapter. We're asked to list three words that someone close to us in this area would use to describe us at our best. Using the same example about my daughter, I listed: *present, engaged, generously loving*. These are the words I'd want my daughter to say about me. Then we take it further by defining each one with a sentence. *I was always present physically and mentally for the important moments in Avery's life. She knew she had my full attention.*

I hope you're having as much fun with this as I am. We're getting to write the story we want. And as I share some of my story, I get fired up and inspired to make it a reality. The same will happen for you as you create each chapter.

The next section in your chapter is composed of three parts. We write a few sentences assessing our current reality in this area. I'll be honest, this may be one of the least fun parts of this process, but we'll never get where we want to go without first knowing where we are. Then it gets a bit more fun by writing where we want to be a year from now. As you're writing this part, I hope you're seeing how real this exercise is.

If you were honest, you just wrote a present reality that is forever sealed in your life story. Now you're deciding where you want to be in a year. This is no longer an exercise. This is your life story. We finish this part of each chapter by writing the most aspirational and inspiring sentence that describes where we will be at the end of our life, assuming we have lived the story we most desired.

Each year, you'll come back and write these three parts again, and over a lifetime this will complete your story. This is the reality of the mark you've left in each chapter of your life. The next step in each chapter is telling the world and ourselves how we made the sentences we wrote about next year become a reality. Remember, we're writing this story as if it already happened. *When we mentally put ourselves in the future we are able to look back on our lives, and it's easier to recognize the commitments we need to make in order to get where we want to go when looking back.*

The next phase in writing our chapters is called Goals and Guardrails. We'll go into more depth on goals and guardrails later as we create our action plan. We repeat the exercise of writing a chapter for each one of our priorities. The flow is the same, and we're creating a consistent rhythm to our story. As you write each chapter, you are creating the plan and storyline you want for your life. Here are 4 tips to keep in mind as you write each chapter:

1. **Don't think, just write.** One of the biggest challenges writers face is thinking too much instead of just writing. Any experienced writer knows that before they publish their book it will undergo multiple rounds of editing, revising and rewriting. You will quickly learn the hardest part in penning your story is just getting your initial thoughts down on paper. If you were to read my first drafts, you'd laugh. I bank on the editing process to bring clarity to the raw cut of my initial thoughts. So just write. Edit later.

2. **Go with your gut.** When you're thinking about what to write in each chapter, go with your gut. Often it's our initial reaction that is the truest. We have to learn to trust ourselves as we move through life. Learning to lean into our gut can be one of the most beneficial things we ever master.

3. **Be honest.** As you're writing, be honest in assessing yourself. You never have to show this to anyone if you feel embarrassed. We will all feel embarrassed in some parts of our story. Honesty is the key to plotting the correct course that leads us where we want to be.

4. **Be aspirational.** Most of what you're writing is meant to be aspirational. It's giving you the ability to **step out of reality for a second and dream about where you want to go**. Don't limit yourself at this stage of the process. Dream big.

You have one life to live. You should be able to live it the way you want. This is your story. It's your life. Don't let fear hold you back from writing it the way you want it to be. As you write the chapters of your life, you will gain the perspective you need to make them a reality. Write your chapters today! Remember, either way, chapters are being written. The only question is, *are you writing them for yourself or are you allowing chance to write them for you?*

Application: *Complete a "Chapter" for each of the priorities you created in the previous section. Use your list of priorities to create the title for each chapter. The "Chapters" section starts on page 30.*

Lesson 5: Goals

Instructions: *Read the lesson and complete the section inside of each Chapter titled "Goals."*
The first "Goals" section is on page 32.

How amazing would it be if we could write something about the present condition of any key area in our life along with a few sentences describing where we wanted to be in a year? And then magically, a year later it happened? Over the course of my life, I've seen people do countless exercises similar to what I've asked you to do: write your current state and follow it up by writing your desired state. I'm not the first person to think of this, and it's used often because it works. However, I've also seen countless people stop there. They get a glimpse of the future they want to create, feel the rush of endorphins, and think, "I've got this." They skip past the next few exercises, brushing them off as things for "other people to do." They shortchange the process, only to fail later and wonder why it didn't work. It didn't work because the process was shortchanged.

We have to create an action plan to go along with our story. If we don't, the story we write will never come to pass, because we didn't take the time to put a plan in place to accomplish it. Have you ever shortchanged a process? If not, then I'm sure you've watched someone else get a piece of instruction and impatiently fail to listen to everything the instructor was saying. They start moving forward only to stop and find themselves coming back for instruction later. The best example I have of this is my daughter. She's pretty independent, so this has happened countless times. When she was three, I began the process of teaching her how to tie her shoes. I had just begun to show her how to cross the laces, and she stopped me and said, "Okay, I got it, Daddy." She ripped the laces out of my hands and proceeded to "tie" her shoes. The only problem being… she had no idea what to do next. She wanted to be independent so badly that, in her zeal, she wouldn't allow me to finish the process of teaching her. This same thing happens to us when it comes to creating goals.

Many of us stop at writing the story we want, and think in our heads that it's obvious what we have to do in order to make it happen. Or we actually do write the goals, but then we aren't willing to entirely commit to the process of walking those goals out for the required period of time. At this point in the *Life Story* process, I've asked you to look at the sentences you've written concerning your present condition.

Then look at the sentences you wrote describing where you'd like to be a year from now, and write the actions you took or would have needed to take to turn those sentences into reality. These actions, steps, or goals are crucial to living the story you're writing. Later on in the process, you'll take the goals you've written down for each section and place them in a chart so you can measure your progress. This is your opportunity to write down every single thing you can think of that you would need to do in order to make the sentences you wrote become a reality. If there's not enough space in the guide, use a separate piece of paper.

The key is to be as specific as possible and write as much as possible. This is your opportunity to get honest with yourself about the commitment you will need to make to create the life you want a year from now.

Sometimes, when we get into this part of the process, we can get nervous that either we can't do all of things it will take or that we can do it but should do more. No matter where you are in the process, you can always go back and edit the sentences you wrote for next year so they'll match what you're willing to commit to. Sometimes, we write those sentences, and then feel guilty about changing them. Don't. Stories get edited and plans gets changed. I would be worried if there weren't edits that needed to be made to your life story. I mention this several times, but I never want anyone to feel guilty about changing their story, commitments, or goals. I'd rather you be realistic about what you can do and achieve it than be unrealistic and put unnecessary pressure on yourself that will only drive you further away from what you truly desire. See this process through and write down everything it will take to make your life story true a year from now.

Application: *Complete the section inside of each Chapter titled "Goals." The first "Goals" section is on page 32.*

Lesson 6: Guardrails

Instructions: *Read the lesson and complete the section inside of each Chapter titled "Guardrails." The first "Guardrails" section is on page 32. Once you've completed each "Guardrails" section, go to page 64 and complete the section titled "Guardrails Time Check."*

Would you like to reduce the risk of being involved in a serious car crash? Of course you would. I knew what a guardrail was when I first created the concept for *Life Story*, but I'd never read the definition. Google defines it as *"a strong fence at the side of a road or the middle of an expressway, intended to reduce the risk of serious accidents."* Merriam-Webster says *"it is a strong metal bar along the side of the road."* Guardrails are meant to save our lives and that's why they are a critical element to consider as we write our story.

For years, I had participated in goal-setting exercises and not once was there a suggestion of implementing the idea of guardrails into the goal-building process. What I did hear was the constant talk of statements like "You'll never wish you spent more time at the office or wish you missed those important family moments." I've seen person after person chasing their dreams of wealth, business, etc. only to lose the things that truly mattered most: family, time, or their health. I've even been guilty of it myself. I'm a hard worker, incredibly persistent, and goal oriented. When I sink my teeth into a goal, I tend not to look up until I'm done and then it's usually too late. I spend quite a bit of time traveling and while I enjoy it, there is a balance. However, in the pursuit of my business goals, it's always been easy to validate every opportunity to travel in order to reach that business or financial goal… so I did.

As Amy and I started to look back on a year in which my travel was pretty intense, we realized that this particular priority in my life had taken over every other one… and it had extended past just a season, it was for a whole year. As we entered the next season of our life, we knew something had to change, so we created guardrails for our goals. **Every priority or chapter in your life story should have guardrails** because if you don't put them in place, you won't know you've gone off the cliff until you're plummeting down it.

In each chapter, I encourage you to do 2 things regarding guardrails. The first is to determine how many hours a week on average you're willing to give this area of your life. Once you've written every chapter, you'll do another exercise that adds up the hours you've committed and shows you what percentage of time you're putting toward each area of your life. When I first did this exercise, I had allocated more hours than there were in a day.

This is common for the first time you try it. As you do this exercise, you have the opportunity to create a time guardrail for each priority of your life. As with everything we do, you won't always be perfect with this, but if you have guardrails you can adjust quickly before you've gone too far and lost something that you truly never wanted to sacrifice.

The next technique in implementing guardrails is when you're asked to write any additional boundaries beyond time. You could have a money guardrail by creating and following a budget. You may have a food-based guardrail like limiting the intake of certain types of foods or a weight-based guardrail to ensure you stay within a healthy range while you achieve your fitness or health goals, and this list can go on and on.

One of the best ways to create guardrails is by asking your significant other or a close friend to help you in the process. I find my wife always knows what my guardrails should be.

Every area of our life needs a safeguard. **Guardrails protect us from getting off track and ultimately losing everything we're working toward.** They create balance in the midst of our largest pursuits. And they help us pre-define how far we're willing to go in the direction of any single pursuit. What you don't do makes way for what you can do. Don't skip over the guardrail exercise when you're writing your life story. Some of the best advice and examples I could give to those watching is a clear playbook on what not to do. Think about how you can start creating guardrails for your life today!

Application: *Complete the section inside of each Chapter titled "Guardrails." The first "Guardrails" section is on page 32. Once you've completed each "Guardrails" section, go to page 64 and complete the section titled "Guardrails Time Check."*

Lesson 7: Life Purpose

Instructions: *Read the lesson and complete the section titled "The Final Chapter: Purpose Statement" on page 60.*

So, what's your purpose? This is one of those questions that can stump us. I've said before that we all fit into one of three buckets when it comes to purpose:

1. We have no clue.
2. We know our purpose, but we can't articulate it.
3. We know it and can articulate it.

No matter which bucket you fit into at the beginning of this exercise, if you've completed the process of writing your life story as I've suggested, you should be able to move to bucket number 3 where you know your purpose thoroughly and can articulate it clearly. Even if you do not know your purpose yet, it has already been mapped out in the lines of the story you've written. Now it's our job is to pull it out.

Here's what I want you to do in order to find your purpose:

1. Look back through the chapters you've written as a part of the *Life Story* exercise. Then, specifically look at the sentences you wrote as the final lines that described that chapter of your life. Re-read each of them and look for a pattern. Have a notepad handy and take notes as you go back through. Why are we doing this? We're doing this because I firmly believe that the purpose of our lives can be found in the story we *want* to write. **When we strip away all ambition and get honest about what story we want to be reading at the end of our life, we find the purest version of ourselves.** And in that version, tucked between the words we wrote, is our purpose. It's a purpose that comes from the heart. Your heart being the core beliefs you hold closest. This whole *Life Story* exercise has been aimed at getting you to strip away the things that don't matter, so you can find the ones that actually do. **Too often, in the middle of our everyday life, we can't discern the difference between what matters and what doesn't**, and that's why putting ourselves in a place of reflection about the end of our life is so powerful.

2. Next, on that notepad you used to look for patterns in the sentences you wrote, create a numbered list that starts at 1 and ends at 1. Yes, I'm serious. Although it sounds ridiculous, it's important. Out of all of the patterns you found, which one is the *one* that depicts the core of your life and who you are? Which *one* sits above the rest?

3. Write why the pattern you chose is the most important in your life.

4. Finally, refine this sentence into a concise description of your purpose.

I'll give you a couple of examples from people who have gone through this process before. I've had several people find that faith is a consistent pattern in their stories.

When they describe the reason why, it all tends to read something like "Faith is most important to me because I believe that true success in my life is all about living my faith out and letting my story give glory to the One I put faith in." Perfect. Now let's take that and create a purpose out of it. Someone who writes these types of notes probably has a purpose that reads something like "My purpose is to give glory to the One I put my faith in." Simple, right?

Your purpose should be simple, not complex. Another pattern I've seen multiple times is family. People will write things like "Family is most important to me because I believe it's my responsibility to leave a legacy through my family. The work I do, the relationships I have all have to do with making my family the priority of my life." Someone like this might determine their purpose would read "My purpose is to provide, teach, and equip my family to grow from generation to generation."

There's no right or wrong purpose, there's only *your purpose*. What patterns did you find while writing your life story? In those patterns lies a purpose. If you haven't already, go back and find it.

Application: *Complete the section titled "The Final Chapter: Purpose Statement" on page 60.*

Lesson 8: Core Values

Instructions: *Read the lesson and complete the section titled "Core Values" on page 61.*

The dictionary describes core values as *"the fundamental belief of a person or organization."* They are the values we hold most dear and make up the core of who we are. This goes for people and companies. Many companies will actually list their core values on their website. They are proud of them. For example, one of the companies I was a part of had the core value "People Over Profit." We'd often talk about it during the interview process and even with potential clients. We wanted everyone to know that we were as committed to people as we were to profit.

So what are your core values? Well, the reality is that we all have them. However, most of us have never *defined* them. And if they're not defined, it can become very easy to "accidentally" not live by them. This is one of the reasons I've included them in *Life Story*. **Just as we should all know our purpose, we should all know our core values.** As you went through the process of writing your life story, you actually did most of the legwork. You were defining your core values without even knowing it. Throughout the guide you filled in blanks using words you'd like to describe each area of your life. Then you described them with a sentence or two. Whether you knew it or not, you were creating the basis for your core values.

The process of sitting down and creating core values can be a bit difficult. Many suggest that you look at a list of hundreds of words and pick the ones that resonate with you the most. Those then become your values. However, I find that process to be difficult and completely out of context. Our values come into play as we live out the chapters of our life story. So they should be created with that in mind. By doing the *Life Story* exercise you created your values. Now it's just a matter of refining them. As you follow the *Life Story* guide, you'll collect all of the words and associated descriptions and place them in the "Core Values" section. Once you've combined the duplicates, the fun part begins. You get to refine and create your core values.

Now, you already know what they are, but there's more to it than that. Although a list of common words and descriptions could be your core values, I've found that if you take it a bit further you're much more likely to use and remember them on a daily basis. So let's refine our core values by making them *memorable*, *short*, and *significant*. Let me give you an example to show you what I mean. One of the values I came up with when doing this exercise was the word "present."

I have a value of being present wherever I am and with whomever I happen to be with. This goes for my family, my career, and myself. I could list the word "present" as one of my values and attach a sentence like: "I will focus on the people, work, or things in front of me in the moment. I will always be in the moment instead of in another moment so that I never find myself missing out." There's nothing wrong with that, but let's take a look at how we could make the same core value memorable, short, and significant.

Memorable. We make it memorable by converting a single word into a short phrase. Just like passwords, a short phrase is easier to remember. Here are a few examples: "Always present." "Eyes on the now." Or "I am here." Those are just a few ways I might take the core value of "present" and make it more memorable.

Short. How do we make it more concise? We shorten the description of our core value by focusing on the part that matters most. I could take the sentence I described above and shorten it to "I will be present everywhere I am." I now have a core value that's memorable and short, which increases the odds that I'll actually remember it.

Significant. Is my value significant enough for me to put it into action? The significance question needs to be asked, after all these are our core values. Ask yourself this: "Would I be satisfied with my life if this statement wasn't true?" Use the answer to determine whether or not your value is significant.

There is not a right or wrong number of core values to have, but I always say it's better to have fewer. If you can condense all of your values into 5 core values, that's amazing because it makes remembering and *acting* easier. However, don't feel bad if you have 10. I consult one company that has 12 and another that has 5. People aren't the same, and since this is personal, it's up to you.

Once you've defined your values, make them a part of your life. Just as a company puts their values on their website, **figure out how to showcase your values**. Some good friends of mine created a piece of art in their house so they would always be reminded. The point is, you don't want to go through the effort of creating your values only to stick them in a folder you never open again. You want to live them every day. So find a way to display your values so that you see them regularly. I would love to hear the creative spin you've taken while creating your core values. Share them with me. I can't wait to read them.

Application: *Complete the section titled "Core Values" on page 61.*

Lesson 9: Checkpoints and Accountability

Instructions: *Read the lesson and complete the section titled "Checkpoints and Accountability" on page 65.*

In order to be successful in achieving the goals you wrote for the upcoming year, you will need checkpoints and accountability along the way. Those who have been around me for any significant amount of time know I harp on these two points constantly. You've put so much work into writing the story you want to live, so I want you to put just as much commitment into ensuring that effort doesn't fall flat. I'll dive into the specifics around what I suggest you do when it comes to checkpoints and accountability as we go along, but let's talk about the "why" for a second.

We need to define the "why" in order to stay focused on our endgame. With time comes distraction, and by having predefined times to check in, we allow ourselves to refocus on what matters.

Stay motivated. It's easy to lose motivation in the middle of writing our story, because we lose perspective on why we're doing it. When we frequently put our "why" back into perspective, we are reminded of how important it is that we stay the course.

Adjust the course. As I've said multiple times, every story has edits and rewrites. Only with time and reviewing that story will those modifications happen. If you never go back and review or allow people to keep you accountable, you'll most likely just end up abandoning your life story instead of editing it.

Kick lazy in the butt. Yes, I said it. We get lazy, all of us. It's nice to have someone to help us kick lazy in the butt, because most of the time we don't actually realize we're being lazy. We make really good excuses that will need an unbiased opinion to uncover.

We need to answer questions like: How will you know whether or not you're making the progress you desire? How will you know when to adjust your story? How will you know if you're getting off course? How will you kick yourself in the butt when you're being lazy? How will you see outside of your own ability to believe in yourself? The answer to all of these is through checkpoints and accountability. Use your Goals and Guardrails Checklist. Or if you have another way of keeping up with what you need to do, use that.

The point of these sheets is to condense the story you've written into easily digestible action plans. Here's what I suggest doing: schedule monthly, quarterly, and yearly checkpoints.

> **Monthly:** Spend at least 30 minutes every month evaluating your progress in the Goals and Guardrails Checklist.

> **Quarterly:** Once a quarter, read back through your life story and adjust specific commitments and goals as necessary.

Annually: Every year go back through the exercise and refine. Make sure to write the following year's steps, goals, and guardrails.

If you have a significant other, do this with them. Amy and I do each one of these checkpoints together or at least at the same time. We also add accountability by finding a person or group of people to connect with on a monthly basis. Use the same process you did before and share your progress using your checklist and any notes you may have written during your time of personal review. Let the person on the other end ask you tough questions and challenge you.

The simple act of having a time scheduled to walk through your progress and hang-ups can be surprisingly effective in keeping you on track, as long as you give that person the permission to be brutally honest. When it comes to selecting a person to keep you accountable, find someone who will be willing to give you a "friendly kick in the butt" if it's needed.

Schedule, schedule, schedule! I've already scheduled my entire year of checkpoints and accountability. It's simple to do, but will ensure it's not an afterthought. Just like any appointment, you can reschedule if something comes up, but the act of scheduling will help you actually do it. **You've written your story. It's begging to be lived.** So start today by putting the right structures in place.

Application: *Read the lesson and complete the section titled "Checkpoints and Accountability" on page 65.*

Lesson 10: The Essentials

Instructions: *Read the lesson and complete the section titled "Life Story: The Essentials" on page 70.*

There's a good chance that if you're reading this, you've completed a first draft of your life story. Congratulations! I want to commend you for taking such a big step toward creating the story you want to live. This story will live with you forever. I still have a piece of paper from an exercise I did like this when I was only fourteen. It was so revolutionary that it has impacted not only my life but my vocational ambitions for the last several decades. I'm convinced that your life story will do the same for you.

As writers, which includes you now, we pour ourselves into the books we write. Every book takes a different amount of time. However, no matter how many pages make up our final manuscript, pieces of ourselves are woven within the pages. Your life story is no different. If you followed the guide as directed, you've probably written around 20 pages or even more. That being said, it's not practical to think that you could read your life story every day. That's why I created "The Essentials."

As I mentioned above, as writers we pour ourselves into our work, and that's one of the reasons many writers have a disdain for CliffsNotes or book summaries sold by others. One, writers don't typically make any money off the sale of these summaries. And two, someone has taken hundreds of pages worth of blood, sweat, and tears and crammed it into a few short pages, removing the heart of the piece. It feels as if your work has been minimized, and maybe in some cases that is true. However, at the same time, there is a lesson here. People love book summaries and are often able to get the most important points from the book without reading the entire thing. Now, I don't believe that reading a summary will get you the same exact value as reading the entire book, but once we have written and read our story, we can ask ourselves the question, what's *essential* when it comes to our life story?

The process of condensing your life story down to the few most important pieces can be painful, but it is always beneficial. I'm going to ask you to decide between priorities. Pick your most important goals and keep these, along with your purpose and life question, at the forefront of your mind. We are going to boil your life story down into one page, and that page is going to be your daily lifeline to answer the question "What matters?" You'll never remember every goal nor take time to think about all ten of your priorities on a daily basis. If you do, more power to you!

I certainly haven't been able to master that one. However, I have been able to master one page of my top priorities. For example, *I currently write every day*. When I wrote my story, I went into depth as to why and how to do this. I know where it fits into my overall goals. However, all that matters on a *daily basis* is whether or not I write.

The good news is you've already done most of the work needed to fill in your Essentials sheet. You now need to determine which goals and guardrails make the cut. Each person's capacity varies, but the fewer things we have on our list, the more likely we are to accomplish them. As you look through your goals and guardrails consider the ones that are most important from each chapter of your life. Write those on a piece of paper.

Do this with both your goals and your guardrails. Next, go back and prioritize the goals and guardrails by the level of importance you've given the chapters they fall under. Finally, pick the ones that you know are most important for you to remember on a daily basis.

This sheet will be a guide that you can look back at before you go to bed and as you plan your day to make sure you're on track with what matters in life. **Today and every day after this you have the power to live the story _you've written_.** So do it, and never look back on your life with regret.

Application: _Complete the section titled "Life Story: The Essentials" on page 70._

The Preface

(Remember that you are now looking back at your life from the future.)

Hi! My name is (*insert your name*) _____. This is the story of my life. As you read my story, you will notice that throughout my life I could always be counted on to/for:

List 1–3 qualities about yourself that you would deem most important if someone else were writing the story of your life. (How do want others to view you?)

_____ (CV),

_____ (CV), and

_____ (CV).

Whether you were to ask a family member or my friends, the three truths above defined the actions I took throughout my life.

Life Question

When I started the process of documenting my life story, I asked myself thoughtful questions on a daily basis. Now, as I look back over my life, I find that one question has been key to keeping me focused on my purpose. This question is what I called my life question. After all, questions drive actions and this question kept me grounded to a life lived with no regrets.

I would suggest everyone have a life question. The question doesn't need to be long and the more direct it is, the better. I created my life question by simply asking myself, "What is the one thing I need to do each day to live out my purpose, priorities, and core values all at once? What question sums it all up?"

Take some time to think through what your life question is and write it in the space below (e.g., What if I lived each day as if it were the last page in my book?). To generate some ideas, try starting with the words: "What if I lived each day…"

My life question has been:

_____

_____.

Note: If you are having a difficult time creating your life question, feel free to skip this section and come back to it later. Also, if you write a question now and then feel like it needs to change later, that's perfectly fine. This is your life story. And, like all great stories, there will be editing, so don't worry about getting it perfect.

Introduction: *What's Important?*

For me, the exercise of nailing down a purpose was challenging. There were so many things I wanted to accomplish in life. It was not for wanting, but more for fear of missing out. I knew that *my purpose was a declaration of who I wanted to be*. This was the one-sentence theme for my life. This is what I wanted the last sentence of the last chapter of my story to say. One of the best ways I've found to think about purpose is by thinking about statements I'd love to have people say about me at my funeral.

For me to understand my life's purpose I had to define the most important aspects of my life. When I determined what was important to me, it became much easier to understand my purpose.

Enter your answers in the blanks below.

The three most important things in my life (*e.g., Faith, Self, Spouse, Children, Career, etc.*):

(1)_____,

(2) _____,

(3) _____.

There was no question about the top three for me. However, the top three weren't the only important parts to my life. There were also more things that were important to me in my life:

There's no right number of priorities. Feel free to do 3 or 23. We can always narrow our focus later. I'll only caution you that the more areas of importance you have, the more your ability to focus will decrease. My areas of importance are Faith, Self, Wife, Kids, Family, Friends, Career.

(4) _____,

(5) _____,

(6) _____,

(7)_____,

(8) _____,

(9) _____,

(10) _____,

These were the areas of my life that deserved attention. I liked to think about each one of these as a chapter in the book of my life starting with the most important and moving down from there. Ranking these priorities was not easy, but the process helped me avoid and resolve conflicts between areas of priority during challenging times. My life could be divided into the following chapters in order of importance:

Review the ranking of your chapters before entering them in order of importance below. Take the time you need to place them in order of importance.

Chapter 1: _____

Chapter 2: _____

Chapter 3: _____

Chapter 4: _____

Chapter 5: _____

Chapter 6: _____

Chapter 7: _____

Chapter 8: _____

Chapter 9: _____

Chapter 10: _____

Chapter 1: _____

Insert Chapter Name from the "Introduction: What's Important?" section of Life Story (page 29).

_____ was important to me because:

Insert Chapter Name.

_____

_____.

In this area of my life, the people that knew me the best would use these words to describe me at my best:

These words define this area of your life. They describe your perfect-case scenario. This exercise will help you define your core values. If you need more words to describe this area, feel free to write them in.

(1) _____ (CV),

(2) _____ (CV),

(3) _____ (CV).

If there were a sentence to describe how I was _____,

Insert answer from line 1 above.

that sentence would be:

_____.

If there were a sentence to describe how I was _____,

Insert answer from line 2 from above.

that sentence would be:

_____.

If there were a sentence to describe how I was _____,

Insert answer from line 3 above.

that sentence would be:

_____.

When I first started writing my story, I decided to examine how I was doing in each area of my life, then I updated where I was each year. Writing the last update was the most rewarding, because I was able to look back over the years of my life and see that *I had written the story I wanted*, instead of letting the story write me. I decided to give myself the task of writing no more than two sentences for each update. It was a bit challenging, but forced me to be honest.

Here are the two sentences that described where I was when I started writing my story (*this is your present reality*). I knew I had to be honest in assessing my present condition if I wanted to plot a course to my future destination:

Insert two sentences that honestly assess where you are right now related to this chapter of your life. If you need to add additional sentences, feel free.

_____

_____

_____

Here are the two sentences I wrote at the end of the first year:

Describe where you want to be in a year. You will repeat this exercise on an annual basis.

_____

_____

_____

Here are the final two sentences I had the privilege to write describing this area of my life:

Write this as your future self after you have written your ideal life story.

_____

_____

_____

Goals

Each year as I wrote my two sentences, I would create an action plan to make my end-of-the-year sentences become reality. The action plan consisted of goals and guardrails. Here's what my action plan looked like the first year.

Note: When we put ourselves in a position to look back on our lives, it's easier to understand the commitments we need to make now in order to get where we want to go. Do this exercise as if you've already reached the goal you're setting for a year from now.

Start with "I was committed to..."

_____ and doing it _____ times (week, month, etc.)

_____ and doing it _____ times (week, month, etc.)

_____ and doing it _____ times (week, month, etc.)

Note: Repeat as many times as needed.

Guardrails

In my pursuit of the above goals, I had to establish "guardrails" to ensure that I gave the appropriate priority to all areas of my life. Just like a guardrail along the highway will keep you from involuntarily off-roading, guardrails in life story planning provide creative constraints.

In budgeting, a guardrail to a savings goal of $100 per month is managing the spending budget for food, clothing, etc.

Time was another type of guardrail I considered. A day is made up of a finite number of hours. When I think about the whole of my life I could only give this chapter _____ hours on average per week without causing damage to the other areas of priority in my life. Beyond the guardrail of time, here are the guardrails that I set in place for this area of my life.

Guardrail: _____

Guardrail: _____

Guardrail: _____

Chapter 2: _____

Insert Chapter Name from the "Introduction: What's Important?" section of Life Story *(page 29).*

_____ was important to me because:

Insert Chapter Name.

_____

_____.

In this area of my life, the people that knew me the best would use these words to describe me at my best:

These words define this area of your life. They describe your perfect-case scenario. This exercise will help you define your core values. If you need more words to describe this area, feel free to write them in.

(1) _____ (CV),

(2) _____ (CV),

(3) _____ (CV).

If there were a sentence to describe how I was _____,

Insert answer from line 1 above.

that sentence would be:

_____.

If there were a sentence to describe how I was _____,

Insert answer from line 2 from above.

that sentence would be:

_____.

If there were a sentence to describe how I was _____,

Insert answer from line 3 above.

that sentence would be:

_____.

When I first started writing my story, I decided to examine how I was doing in each area of my life, then I updated where I was each year. Writing the last update was the most rewarding, because I was able to look back over the years of my life and see that *I had written the story I wanted*, instead of letting the story write me. I decided to give myself the task of writing no more than two sentences for each update. It was a bit challenging, but forced me to be honest.

Here are the two sentences that described where I was when I started writing my story (*this is your present reality*). I knew I had to be honest in assessing my present condition if I wanted to plot a course to my future destination:

Insert two sentences that honestly assess where you are right now related to this chapter of your life. If you need to add additional sentences, feel free.

_____

_____

_____

Here are the two sentences I wrote at the end of the first year:

Describe where you want to be in a year. You will repeat this exercise on an annual basis.

_____

_____

_____

Here are the final two sentences I had the privilege to write describing this area of my life:

Write this as your future self after you have written your ideal life story.

_____

_____

_____

Goals

Each year as I wrote my two sentences, I would create an action plan to make my end-of-the-year sentences become reality. The action plan consisted of goals and guardrails. Here's what my action plan looked like the first year.

Note: When we put ourselves in a position to look back on our lives, it's easier to understand the commitments we need to make now in order to get where we want to go. Do this exercise as if you've already reached the goal you're setting for a year from now.

Start with "I was committed to..."

_____ and doing it _____ times (week, month, etc.)

_____ and doing it _____ times (week, month, etc.)

_____ and doing it _____ times (week, month, etc.)

Note: Repeat as many times as needed.

Guardrails

In my pursuit of the above goals, I had to establish "guardrails" to ensure that I gave the appropriate priority to all areas of my life. Just like a guardrail along the highway will keep you from involuntarily off-roading, guardrails in life story planning provide creative constraints.

In budgeting, a guardrail to a savings goal of $100 per month is managing the spending budget for food, clothing, etc.

Time was another type of guardrail I considered. A day is made up of a finite number of hours. When I think about the whole of my life I could only give this chapter _____ hours on average per week without causing damage to the other areas of priority in my life. Beyond the guardrail of time, here are the guardrails that I set in place for this area of my life.

Guardrail: _____

Guardrail: _____

Guardrail: _____

Chapter 3: _____

Insert Chapter Name from the "Introduction: What's Important?" section of Life Story (page 29).

_____ was important to me because:

Insert Chapter Name.

_____

_____.

In this area of my life, the people that knew me the best would use these words to describe me at my best:

These words define this area of your life. They describe your perfect-case scenario. This exercise will help you define your core values. If you need more words to describe this area, feel free to write them in.

(1) _____ (CV),

(2) _____ (CV),

(3) _____ (CV).

If there were a sentence to describe how I was _____,

Insert answer from line 1 above.

that sentence would be:

_____.

If there were a sentence to describe how I was _____,

Insert answer from line 2 from above.

that sentence would be:

_____.

If there were a sentence to describe how I was _____,

Insert answer from line 3 above.

that sentence would be:

_____.

When I first started writing my story, I decided to examine how I was doing in each area of my life, then I updated where I was each year. Writing the last update was the most rewarding, because I was able to look back over the years of my life and see that *I had written the story I wanted*, instead of letting the story write me. I decided to give myself the task of writing no more than two sentences for each update. It was a bit challenging, but forced me to be honest.

Here are the two sentences that described where I was when I started writing my story (*this is your present reality*). I knew I had to be honest in assessing my present condition if I wanted to plot a course to my future destination:

Insert two sentences that honestly assess where you are right now related to this chapter of your life. If you need to add additional sentences, feel free.

_____

_____

_____

Here are the two sentences I wrote at the end of the first year:

Describe where you want to be in a year. You will repeat this exercise on an annual basis.

_____

_____

_____

Here are the final two sentences I had the privilege to write describing this area of my life:

Write this as your future self after you have written your ideal life story.

_____

_____

_____

Goals

Each year as I wrote my two sentences, I would create an action plan to make my end-of-the-year sentences become reality. The action plan consisted of goals and guardrails. Here's what my action plan looked like the first year.

Note: When we put ourselves in a position to look back on our lives, it's easier to understand the commitments we need to make now in order to get where we want to go. Do this exercise as if you've already reached the goal you're setting for a year from now.

Start with "I was committed to..."

_____ and doing it _____ times (week, month, etc.)

_____ and doing it _____ times (week, month, etc.)

_____ and doing it _____ times (week, month, etc.)

Note: Repeat as many times as needed.

Guardrails

In my pursuit of the above goals, I had to establish "guardrails" to ensure that I gave the appropriate priority to all areas of my life. Just like a guardrail along the highway will keep you from involuntarily off-roading, guardrails in life story planning provide creative constraints.

In budgeting, a guardrail to a savings goal of $100 per month is managing the spending budget for food, clothing, etc.

Time was another type of guardrail I considered. A day is made up of a finite number of hours. When I think about the whole of my life I could only give this chapter _____ hours on average per week without causing damage to the other areas of priority in my life. Beyond the guardrail of time, here are the guardrails that I set in place for this area of my life.

Guardrail: _____

Guardrail: _____

Guardrail: _____

Chapter 4: _____

Insert Chapter Name from the "Introduction: What's Important?" section of Life Story (page 29).

_____ was important to me because:

Insert Chapter Name.

_____

_____.

In this area of my life, the people that knew me the best would use these words to describe me at my best:

These words define this area of your life. They describe your perfect-case scenario. This exercise will help you define your core values. If you need more words to describe this area, feel free to write them in.

(1) _____ (CV),

(2) _____ (CV),

(3) _____ (CV).

If there were a sentence to describe how I was _____,

Insert answer from line 1 above.

that sentence would be:

_____.

If there were a sentence to describe how I was _____,

Insert answer from line 2 from above.

that sentence would be:

_____.

If there were a sentence to describe how I was _____,

Insert answer from line 3 above.

that sentence would be:

_____.

When I first started writing my story, I decided to examine how I was doing in each area of my life, then I updated where I was each year. Writing the last update was the most rewarding, because I was able to look back over the years of my life and see that *I had written the story I wanted*, instead of letting the story write me. I decided to give myself the task of writing no more than two sentences for each update. It was a bit challenging, but forced me to be honest.

Here are the two sentences that described where I was when I started writing my story (*this is your present reality*). I knew I had to be honest in assessing my present condition if I wanted to plot a course to my future destination:

Insert two sentences that honestly assess where you are right now related to this chapter of your life. If you need to add additional sentences, feel free.

_____

_____

_____

Here are the two sentences I wrote at the end of the first year:

Describe where you want to be in a year. You will repeat this exercise on an annual basis.

_____

_____

_____

Here are the final two sentences I had the privilege to write describing this area of my life:

Write this as your future self after you have written your ideal life story.

_____

_____

_____

Goals

Each year as I wrote my two sentences, I would create an action plan to make my end-of-the-year sentences become reality. The action plan consisted of goals and guardrails. Here's what my action plan looked like the first year.

Note: When we put ourselves in a position to look back on our lives, it's easier to understand the commitments we need to make now in order to get where we want to go. Do this exercise as if you've already reached the goal you're setting for a year from now.

Start with "I was committed to…"

_____ and doing it _____ times (week, month, etc.)

_____ and doing it _____ times (week, month, etc.)

_____ and doing it _____ times (week, month, etc.)

Note: Repeat as many times as needed.

Guardrails

In my pursuit of the above goals, I had to establish "guardrails" to ensure that I gave the appropriate priority to all areas of my life. Just like a guardrail along the highway will keep you from involuntarily off-roading, guardrails in life story planning provide creative constraints.

In budgeting, a guardrail to a savings goal of $100 per month is managing the spending budget for food, clothing, etc.

Time was another type of guardrail I considered. A day is made up of a finite number of hours. When I think about the whole of my life I could only give this chapter _____ hours on average per week without causing damage to the other areas of priority in my life. Beyond the guardrail of time, here are the guardrails that I set in place for this area of my life.

Guardrail: _____

Guardrail: _____

Guardrail: _____

Chapter 5: _____

Insert Chapter Name from the "Introduction: What's Important?" section of Life Story (page 29).

_____ was important to me because:

Insert Chapter Name.

_____

_____.

In this area of my life, the people that knew me the best would use these words to describe me at my best:

These words define this area of your life. They describe your perfect-case scenario. This exercise will help you define your core values. If you need more words to describe this area, feel free to write them in.

(1) _____ (CV),

(2) _____ (CV),

(3) _____ (CV).

If there were a sentence to describe how I was _____,

Insert answer from line 1 above.

that sentence would be:

_____.

If there were a sentence to describe how I was _____,

Insert answer from line 2 from above.

that sentence would be:

_____.

If there were a sentence to describe how I was _____,

Insert answer from line 3 above.

that sentence would be:

_____.

When I first started writing my story, I decided to examine how I was doing in each area of my life, then I updated where I was each year. Writing the last update was the most rewarding, because I was able to look back over the years of my life and see that *I had written the story I wanted*, instead of letting the story write me. I decided to give myself the task of writing no more than two sentences for each update. It was a bit challenging, but forced me to be honest.

Here are the two sentences that described where I was when I started writing my story (*this is your present reality*). I knew I had to be honest in assessing my present condition if I wanted to plot a course to my future destination:

Insert two sentences that honestly assess where you are right now related to this chapter of your life. If you need to add additional sentences, feel free.

_____

_____

_____

Here are the two sentences I wrote at the end of the first year:

Describe where you want to be in a year. You will repeat this exercise on an annual basis.

_____

_____

_____

Here are the final two sentences I had the privilege to write describing this area of my life:

Write this as your future self after you have written your ideal life story.

_____

_____

_____

Goals

Each year as I wrote my two sentences, I would create an action plan to make my end-of-the-year sentences become reality. The action plan consisted of goals and guardrails. Here's what my action plan looked like the first year.

Note: When we put ourselves in a position to look back on our lives, it's easier to understand the commitments we need to make now in order to get where we want to go. Do this exercise as if you've already reached the goal you're setting for a year from now.

Start with "I was committed to…"

_____ and doing it _____ times (week, month, etc.)

_____ and doing it _____ times (week, month, etc.)

_____ and doing it _____ times (week, month, etc.)

Note: Repeat as many times as needed.

Guardrails

In my pursuit of the above goals, I had to establish "guardrails" to ensure that I gave the appropriate priority to all areas of my life. Just like a guardrail along the highway will keep you from involuntarily off-roading, guardrails in life story planning provide creative constraints.

In budgeting, a guardrail to a savings goal of $100 per month is managing the spending budget for food, clothing, etc.

Time was another type of guardrail I considered. A day is made up of a finite number of hours. When I think about the whole of my life I could only give this chapter _____ hours on average per week without causing damage to the other areas of priority in my life. Beyond the guardrail of time, here are the guardrails that I set in place for this area of my life.

Guardrail: _____

Guardrail: _____

Guardrail: _____

Chapter 6: _____

Insert Chapter Name from the "Introduction: What's Important?" section of Life Story (page 29).

_____ was important to me because:

Insert Chapter Name.

_____

_____.

In this area of my life, the people that knew me the best would use these words to describe me at my best:

These words define this area of your life. They describe your perfect-case scenario. This exercise will help you define your core values. If you need more words to describe this area, feel free to write them in.

(1) _____ (CV),

(2) _____ (CV),

(3) _____ (CV).

If there were a sentence to describe how I was _____,

Insert answer from line 1 above.

that sentence would be:

_____.

If there were a sentence to describe how I was _____,

Insert answer from line 2 from above.

that sentence would be:

_____.

If there were a sentence to describe how I was _____,

Insert answer from line 3 above.

that sentence would be:

_____.

When I first started writing my story, I decided to examine how I was doing in each area of my life, then I updated where I was each year. Writing the last update was the most rewarding, because I was able to look back over the years of my life and see that *I had written the story I wanted*, instead of letting the story write me. I decided to give myself the task of writing no more than two sentences for each update. It was a bit challenging, but forced me to be honest.

Here are the two sentences that described where I was when I started writing my story (*this is your present reality*). I knew I had to be honest in assessing my present condition if I wanted to plot a course to my future destination:

Insert two sentences that honestly assess where you are right now related to this chapter of your life. If you need to add additional sentences, feel free.

_____

_____

_____

Here are the two sentences I wrote at the end of the first year:

Describe where you want to be in a year. You will repeat this exercise on an annual basis.

_____

_____

_____

Here are the final two sentences I had the privilege to write describing this area of my life:

Write this as your future self after you have written your ideal life story.

_____

_____

_____

Goals

Each year as I wrote my two sentences, I would create an action plan to make my end-of-the-year sentences become reality. The action plan consisted of goals and guardrails. Here's what my action plan looked like the first year.

Note: When we put ourselves in a position to look back on our lives, it's easier to understand the commitments we need to make now in order to get where we want to go. Do this exercise as if you've already reached the goal you're setting for a year from now.

Start with "I was committed to…"

_____ and doing it _____ times (week, month, etc.)

_____ and doing it _____ times (week, month, etc.)

_____ and doing it _____ times (week, month, etc.)

Note: Repeat as many times as needed.

Guardrails

In my pursuit of the above goals, I had to establish "guardrails" to ensure that I gave the appropriate priority to all areas of my life. Just like a guardrail along the highway will keep you from involuntarily off-roading, guardrails in life story planning provide creative constraints.

In budgeting, a guardrail to a savings goal of $100 per month is managing the spending budget for food, clothing, etc.

Time was another type of guardrail I considered. A day is made up of a finite number of hours. When I think about the whole of my life I could only give this chapter _____ hours on average per week without causing damage to the other areas of priority in my life. Beyond the guardrail of time, here are the guardrails that I set in place for this area of my life.

Guardrail: _____

Guardrail: _____

Guardrail: _____

Chapter 7: _____

Insert Chapter Name from the "Introduction: What's Important?" section of Life Story *(page 29).*

_____ was important to me because:

Insert Chapter Name.

_____

_____.

In this area of my life, the people that knew me the best would use these words to describe me at my best:

These words define this area of your life. They describe your perfect-case scenario. This exercise will help you define your core values. If you need more words to describe this area, feel free to write them in.

(1) _____ (CV),

(2) _____ (CV),

(3) _____ (CV).

If there were a sentence to describe how I was _____,

Insert answer from line 1 above.

that sentence would be:

_____.

If there were a sentence to describe how I was _____,

Insert answer from line 2 from above.

that sentence would be:

_____.

If there were a sentence to describe how I was _____,

Insert answer from line 3 above.

that sentence would be:

_____.

When I first started writing my story, I decided to examine how I was doing in each area of my life, then I updated where I was each year. Writing the last update was the most rewarding, because I was able to look back over the years of my life and see that *I had written the story I wanted*, instead of letting the story write me. I decided to give myself the task of writing no more than two sentences for each update. It was a bit challenging, but forced me to be honest.

Here are the two sentences that described where I was when I started writing my story (*this is your present reality*). I knew I had to be honest in assessing my present condition if I wanted to plot a course to my future destination:

Insert two sentences that honestly assess where you are right now related to this chapter of your life. If you need to add additional sentences, feel free.

_____

_____

_____

Here are the two sentences I wrote at the end of the first year:

Describe where you want to be in a year. You will repeat this exercise on an annual basis.

_____

_____

_____

Here are the final two sentences I had the privilege to write describing this area of my life:

Write this as your future self after you have written your ideal life story.

_____

_____

_____

Goals

Each year as I wrote my two sentences, I would create an action plan to make my end-of-the-year sentences become reality. The action plan consisted of goals and guardrails. Here's what my action plan looked like the first year.

Note: When we put ourselves in a position to look back on our lives, it's easier to understand the commitments we need to make now in order to get where we want to go. Do this exercise as if you've already reached the goal you're setting for a year from now.

Start with "I was committed to…"

_____ and doing it _____ times (week, month, etc.)

_____ and doing it _____ times (week, month, etc.)

_____ and doing it _____ times (week, month, etc.)

Note: Repeat as many times as needed.

Guardrails

In my pursuit of the above goals, I had to establish "guardrails" to ensure that I gave the appropriate priority to all areas of my life. Just like a guardrail along the highway will keep you from involuntarily off-roading, guardrails in life story planning provide creative constraints.

In budgeting, a guardrail to a savings goal of $100 per month is managing the spending budget for food, clothing, etc.

Time was another type of guardrail I considered. A day is made up of a finite number of hours. When I think about the whole of my life I could only give this chapter _____ hours on average per week without causing damage to the other areas of priority in my life. Beyond the guardrail of time, here are the guardrails that I set in place for this area of my life.

Guardrail: _____

Guardrail: _____

Guardrail: _____

Chapter 8: _____

Insert Chapter Name from the "Introduction: What's Important?" section of Life Story *(page 29).*

_____ was important to me because:

Insert Chapter Name.

_____

_____.

In this area of my life, the people that knew me the best would use these words to describe me at my best:

These words define this area of your life. They describe your perfect-case scenario. This exercise will help you define your core values. If you need more words to describe this area, feel free to write them in.

(1) _____ (CV),

(2) _____ (CV),

(3) _____ (CV).

If there were a sentence to describe how I was _____,

Insert answer from line 1 above.

that sentence would be:

_____.

If there were a sentence to describe how I was _____,

Insert answer from line 2 from above.

that sentence would be:

_____.

If there were a sentence to describe how I was _____,

Insert answer from line 3 above.

that sentence would be:

_____.

When I first started writing my story, I decided to examine how I was doing in each area of my life, then I updated where I was each year. Writing the last update was the most rewarding, because I was able to look back over the years of my life and see that *I had written the story I wanted*, instead of letting the story write me. I decided to give myself the task of writing no more than two sentences for each update. It was a bit challenging, but forced me to be honest.

Here are the two sentences that described where I was when I started writing my story (*this is your present reality*). I knew I had to be honest in assessing my present condition if I wanted to plot a course to my future destination:

Insert two sentences that honestly assess where you are right now related to this chapter of your life. If you need to add additional sentences, feel free.

_____

_____

_____

Here are the two sentences I wrote at the end of the first year:

Describe where you want to be in a year. You will repeat this exercise on an annual basis.

_____

_____

_____

Here are the final two sentences I had the privilege to write describing this area of my life:

Write this as your future self after you have written your ideal life story.

_____

_____

_____

Goals

Each year as I wrote my two sentences, I would create an action plan to make my end-of-the-year sentences become reality. The action plan consisted of goals and guardrails. Here's what my action plan looked like the first year.

Note: When we put ourselves in a position to look back on our lives, it's easier to understand the commitments we need to make now in order to get where we want to go. Do this exercise as if you've already reached the goal you're setting for a year from now.

Start with "I was committed to…"

_____ and doing it _____ times (week, month, etc.)

_____ and doing it _____ times (week, month, etc.)

_____ and doing it _____ times (week, month, etc.)

Note: Repeat as many times as needed.

Guardrails

In my pursuit of the above goals, I had to establish "guardrails" to ensure that I gave the appropriate priority to all areas of my life. Just like a guardrail along the highway will keep you from involuntarily off-roading, guardrails in life story planning provide creative constraints.

In budgeting, a guardrail to a savings goal of $100 per month is managing the spending budget for food, clothing, etc.

Time was another type of guardrail I considered. A day is made up of a finite number of hours. When I think about the whole of my life I could only give this chapter _____ hours on average per week without causing damage to the other areas of priority in my life. Beyond the guardrail of time, here are the guardrails that I set in place for this area of my life.

Guardrail: _____

Guardrail: _____

Guardrail: _____

Chapter 9: _____

Insert Chapter Name from the "Introduction: What's Important?" section of Life Story *(page 29).*

_____ was important to me because:

Insert Chapter Name.

_____

_____.

In this area of my life, the people that knew me the best would use these words to describe me at my best:

These words define this area of your life. They describe your perfect-case scenario. This exercise will help you define your core values. If you need more words to describe this area, feel free to write them in.

(1) _____ (CV),

(2) _____ (CV),

(3) _____ (CV).

If there were a sentence to describe how I was _____,

Insert answer from line 1 above.

that sentence would be:

_____.

If there were a sentence to describe how I was _____,

Insert answer from line 2 from above.

that sentence would be:

_____.

If there were a sentence to describe how I was _____,

Insert answer from line 3 above.

that sentence would be:

_____.

When I first started writing my story, I decided to examine how I was doing in each area of my life, then I updated where I was each year. Writing the last update was the most rewarding, because I was able to look back over the years of my life and see that *I had written the story I wanted*, instead of letting the story write me. I decided to give myself the task of writing no more than two sentences for each update. It was a bit challenging, but forced me to be honest.

Here are the two sentences that described where I was when I started writing my story (*this is your present reality*). I knew I had to be honest in assessing my present condition if I wanted to plot a course to my future destination:

Insert two sentences that honestly assess where you are right now related to this chapter of your life. If you need to add additional sentences, feel free.

_____

_____

_____

Here are the two sentences I wrote at the end of the first year:

Describe where you want to be in a year. You will repeat this exercise on an annual basis.

_____

_____

_____

Here are the final two sentences I had the privilege to write describing this area of my life:

Write this as your future self after you have written your ideal life story.

_____

_____

_____

Goals

Each year as I wrote my two sentences, I would create an action plan to make my end-of-the-year sentences become reality. The action plan consisted of goals and guardrails. Here's what my action plan looked like the first year.

Note: When we put ourselves in a position to look back on our lives, it's easier to understand the commitments we need to make now in order to get where we want to go. Do this exercise as if you've already reached the goal you're setting for a year from now.

Start with "I was committed to…"

_____ and doing it _____ times (week, month, etc.)

_____ and doing it _____ times (week, month, etc.)

_____ and doing it _____ times (week, month, etc.)

Note: Repeat as many times as needed.

Guardrails

In my pursuit of the above goals, I had to establish "guardrails" to ensure that I gave the appropriate priority to all areas of my life. Just like a guardrail along the highway will keep you from involuntarily off-roading, guardrails in life story planning provide creative constraints.

In budgeting, a guardrail to a savings goal of $100 per month is managing the spending budget for food, clothing, etc.

Time was another type of guardrail I considered. A day is made up of a finite number of hours. When I think about the whole of my life I could only give this chapter _____ hours on average per week without causing damage to the other areas of priority in my life. Beyond the guardrail of time, here are the guardrails that I set in place for this area of my life.

Guardrail: _____

Guardrail: _____

Guardrail: _____

Chapter 10: _____

Insert Chapter Name from the "Introduction: What's Important?" section of Life Story *(page 29).*

_____ was important to me because:

Insert Chapter Name.

_____

_____.

In this area of my life, the people that knew me the best would use these words to describe me at my best: .

These words define this area of your life. They describe your perfect-case scenario. This exercise will help you define your core values. If you need more words to describe this area, feel free to write them in.

(1) _____ (CV),

(2) _____ (CV),

(3) _____ (CV).

If there were a sentence to describe how I was _____,

Insert answer from line 1 above.

that sentence would be:

_____.

If there were a sentence to describe how I was _____,

Insert answer from line 2 from above.

that sentence would be:

_____.

If there were a sentence to describe how I was _____,

Insert answer from line 3 above.

that sentence would be:

_____.

When I first started writing my story, I decided to examine how I was doing in each area of my life, then I updated where I was each year. Writing the last update was the most rewarding, because I was able to look back over the years of my life and see that *I had written the story I wanted*, instead of letting the story write me. I decided to give myself the task of writing no more than two sentences for each update. It was a bit challenging, but forced me to be honest.

Here are the two sentences that described where I was when I started writing my story (*this is your present reality*). I knew I had to be honest in assessing my present condition if I wanted to plot a course to my future destination:

Insert two sentences that honestly assess where you are right now related to this chapter of your life. If you need to add additional sentences, feel free.

_____

_____

_____

Here are the two sentences I wrote at the end of the first year:

Describe where you want to be in a year. You will repeat this exercise on an annual basis.

_____

_____

_____

Here are the final two sentences I had the privilege to write describing this area of my life:

Write this as your future self after you have written your ideal life story.

_____

_____

_____

Goals

Each year as I wrote my two sentences, I would create an action plan to make my end-of-the-year sentences become reality. The action plan consisted of goals and guardrails. Here's what my action plan looked like the first year.

Note: When we put ourselves in a position to look back on our lives, it's easier to understand the commitments we need to make now in order to get where we want to go. Do this exercise as if you've already reached the goal you're setting for a year from now.

Start with "I was committed to…"

_____ and doing it _____ times (week, month, etc.)

_____ and doing it _____ times (week, month, etc.)

_____ and doing it _____ times (week, month, etc.)

Note: Repeat as many times as needed.

Guardrails

In my pursuit of the above goals, I had to establish "guardrails" to ensure that I gave the appropriate priority to all areas of my life. Just like a guardrail along the highway will keep you from involuntarily off-roading, guardrails in life story planning provide creative constraints.

In budgeting, a guardrail to a savings goal of $100 per month is managing the spending budget for food, clothing, etc.

Time was another type of guardrail I considered. A day is made up of a finite number of hours. When I think about the whole of my life I could only give this chapter _____ hours on average per week without causing damage to the other areas of priority in my life. Beyond the guardrail of time, here are the guardrails that I set in place for this area of my life.

Guardrail: _____

Guardrail: _____

Guardrail: _____

The Final Chapter: *Purpose Statement*

As I reflect back over the story I've written for my life, I'm thankful that I took the time to be intentional about crafting it along the way. This allowed me to write it the way I wanted instead of the way my emotions, personal relationships, or circumstances dictated. When I sum up the story of my life, I sum it up with one sentence. That sentence is my purpose and it reads like this:

_____

_____.

This is my story. It's the story of my life. A story I'm proud to have written.

Core Values

Go back through your life story and use your answers to fill in the following blanks. Anytime you see the initials "CV" by a blank, add the word in that blank to the worksheet below. Anytime you wrote a description of one of the words in the blank, copy it into the appropriate section below. If you weren't prompted to write a sentence with one of the core values, please do it now.

Once you've finished the above, you should have a list of potential core values along with sentences to describe most of them.

Use the following steps to create and refine your core values:

1. Combine duplicates. There's a good chance you used the same word or a similar word to describe yourself throughout the story. That's great! Take a moment to come up with a singular word or short phrase to describe the duplicates. Then do the same thing for the description of each.
2. Once you have a combined list of potential core values, look through the list and cross out anything that doesn't align with what you want your core values to be.
3. If there is a word or short phrase that describes something you didn't write in the story but you believe should be a core value, add it in one of the blanks below.
4. Now you should have a draft of your core values. Take time to look back through each one and refine it. I suggest taking the words you've used to describe your core values along with the descriptive sentences to create a unique core value statement. For example, if the word "dependable" was one of your core values, you might refine it to say: "You can count on me." Your description might be: "I'm a person that can be counted on to come through when it's important." I've found that this exercise can make your core values both more memorable and personal.

CV (Core Value 1): _____

Description: _____

_____.

Refined Core Value: _____

CV (Core Value 2): _____

Description: _____

_____.

Refined Core Value: _____

CV (Core Value 3): _____

Description: _____

_____.

Refined Core Value: _____

CV (Core Value 4): _____

Description: _____

_____.

Refined Core Value: _____

CV (Core Value 5): _____

Description: _____

_____.

Refined Core Value: _____

CV (Core Value 6): _____

Description: _____

_____.

Refined Core Value: _____

CV (Core Value 7): _____

Description: _____

_____.

Refined Core Value: _____

CV (Core Value 8): _____

Description: _____

_____ .

Refined Core Value: _____

CV (Core Value 9): _____

Description: _____

_____ .

Refined Core Value: _____

CV (Core Value 10): _____

Description: _____

_____ .

Refined Core Value: _____

CV (Core Value 11): _____

Description: _____

_____ .

Refined Core Value: _____

Guardrails Time Check

You've created several guardrails throughout the course of writing your life story. Guardrails are important because they provide pre-defined limits that allow you to accomplish the whole of what you want to achieve in your life. In the exercise below, we will look at the amount of time you've budgeted for each area of your life to make sure you haven't budgeted more time than is physically possible.

Life Chapters	Hours/Week	% of Time (___ hours/168)
Example: Family	20	12%

Misc: Use this to include areas such as eating or sleeping that may not have been accounted for. A good average is 10 hours per day, but adjust as necessary for you.

Total

Once you've added up the totals from all areas of your life, compare the totals with the actual numbers of hours in a week. Are your guardrails realistic? If not, go back through each area in your life and make adjustments. You may have to tighten your guardrails in some areas to ensure time to meet all of your priorities. I always recommend increasing time on your top priorities and decreasing time from your bottom priorities.

Then, go back through your life story and list all of your guardrails in the Goals and Guardrails Checklist. This will give you a comprehensive list of limits you need in your life and a place to stay accountable to them.

Checkpoints and Accountability

In order to be successful in achieving the goals you wrote for the following year, you have to have checkpoints and accountability.

Monthly Checkpoint

Go back through the Goals and Guardrails you've created for the chapters of your life story and list them in the Goals and Guardrails Checklist on the following pages. Fill in each table from highest priority area (first chapter) to lowest priority area (last chapter). This will serve as your checklist. Feel free to duplicate this table as many times as needed.

Then use the Goals and Guardrails Checklist on the following pages to keep track of your progress. Use the words "yes," "no," or "some" to denote how you performed in a given period. Fill in the notes to add context, tips for yourself, or anything you think may be helpful to look back on.

Finally, spend at least 15 minutes every month evaluating your progress in the Goals and Guardrails Checklist.

Accountability

I also know that I need to share my progress with someone who can keep me accountable. That person is _____. I'll schedule at least _____ hour(s) every month with them to touch base on my progress and allow them to challenge me.

Quarterly Checkpoint

Once a quarter, read back through your life story and adjust as needed. Remember, your story will have edits and rewrites, so make time to adjust course as you go.

Yearly Checkpoint

Every year go back through the entire *Life Story* exercise and refine as necessary. Make sure to write the following year's sentences, goals, and guardrails.

Goals and Guardrails Checklist

_____ (Month)	Yes, Some, No	Notes
Example: Write 2x per week	Yes	Did great. Didn't miss a day.

Goals and Guardrails Checklist

_____ (Month)   Yes, Some, No   Notes

Goals and Guardrails Checklist

_____ (Month)   Yes, Some, No   Notes

Goals and Guardrails Checklist

_____ (Month)   Yes, Some, No   Notes

Life Story: *The Essentials*

The essentials are what you need to focus on now. They are the most important items from your life story. This one-page overview is something that you can carry with you or refer to on a daily basis to ensure you are writing the story you desire for your life.

My purpose is (*insert your purpose*):

_____.

I keep my purpose at the forefront of my mind by daily asking myself (*insert life question*):

_____.

The most important areas of my life are (*insert top 3 areas of priority*):

(1) _____ (2) _____ (3) _____

When I consider the most important areas of my life (listed above), my highest priority goals/commitments for the following year are (*list the most important goals/commitments in your life*):

(1) _____ (2) _____ (3) _____

(4) _____ (5) _____ (6) _____

When I consider the most important areas of my life (listed above), I must respect the following guardrails (*insert the most important guardrails*):

(1) _____ (2) _____ (3) _____

About Chris Capehart

"My dad was a pastor and cheated on my mom.
She committed suicide.
He died of cancer.
I defied the odds and so can you."

Chris's story is proof that though life rarely gives us what we hope for, we can still beat the odds and achieve a meaningful life. Every challenge presents a choice; a choice to either let circumstances define us or to do exactly the opposite. Chris has made it a point to do exactly the opposite by defining his own life and taking purposeful steps to overcome every challenge thrown his way. His fresh approach to overcoming the inevitable challenges life brings will inspire and motivate people from all walks of life to connect with their purpose and move beyond the challenges they face.

His experience of defying the odds stretches beyond overcoming personal challenges and into the business realm. Growing up, Chris worked in the family "startup" business. That startup went on to gross over $200 million. In the years since, Chris has started or had ownership in over 10 businesses, experiencing a wide range of ups and downs; from losing everything to building it all back from scratch.

While serving as CMO at Oven Bits, he drove over 100% growth, adding millions in revenue and helping produce 20+ features in the Apple and Google App Stores. This was done in partnership with brands such as L'Oréal, Lush Cosmetics, Hilton, and Vogue. During this time, Chris published his first book: **Step:** *Pursuing Your Dreams in the Midst of Everyday Life.*

Chris has since produced **Life Story:** *A Step-by-Step Guide to Creating the Life You've Always Wanted,* **The "Blank" Leader:** *An In-Depth Guide to Becoming a Thriving Leader,* and **The Intentional Year:** *A Year Dedicated to Making You Unstoppable.*

Through the exhilarating heights of hard-earned success to the lows of disappointing failures, Chris has learned a handful of key principles that have helped him defeat the odds. He's now on a mission to teach people of all walks of life how they can do the same and defeat the odds no matter what their "everyday life" looks like.

Other Resources

Find all of Chris's resources at ChrisCapehart.co.

Made in the USA
Columbia, SC
26 March 2020